I can tug.

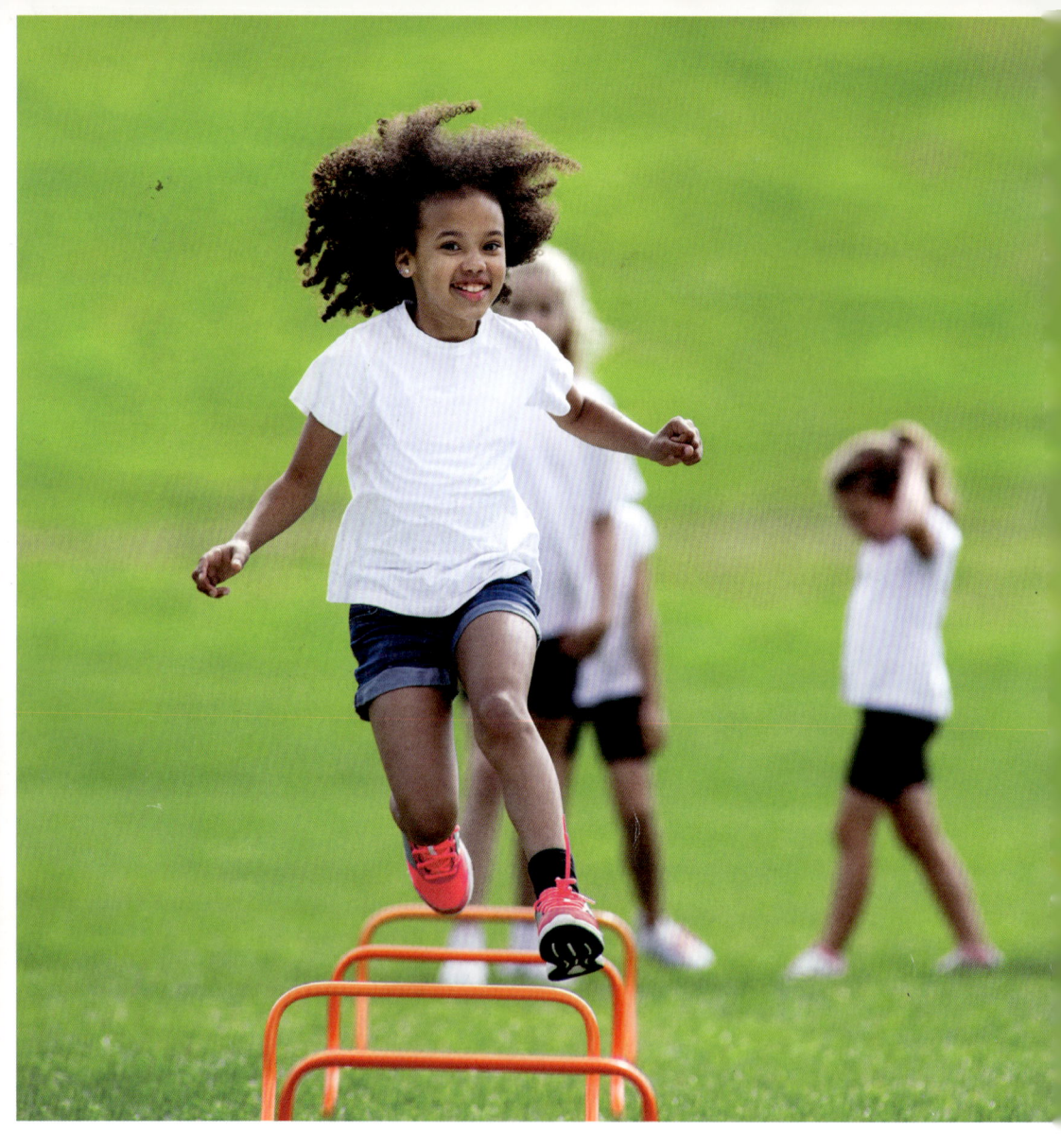

I can run and tug.

I Can Run

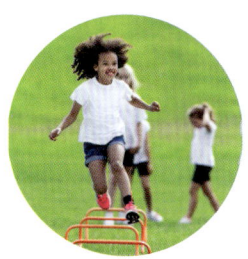

Written by
Stephen Rickard

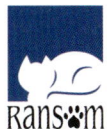

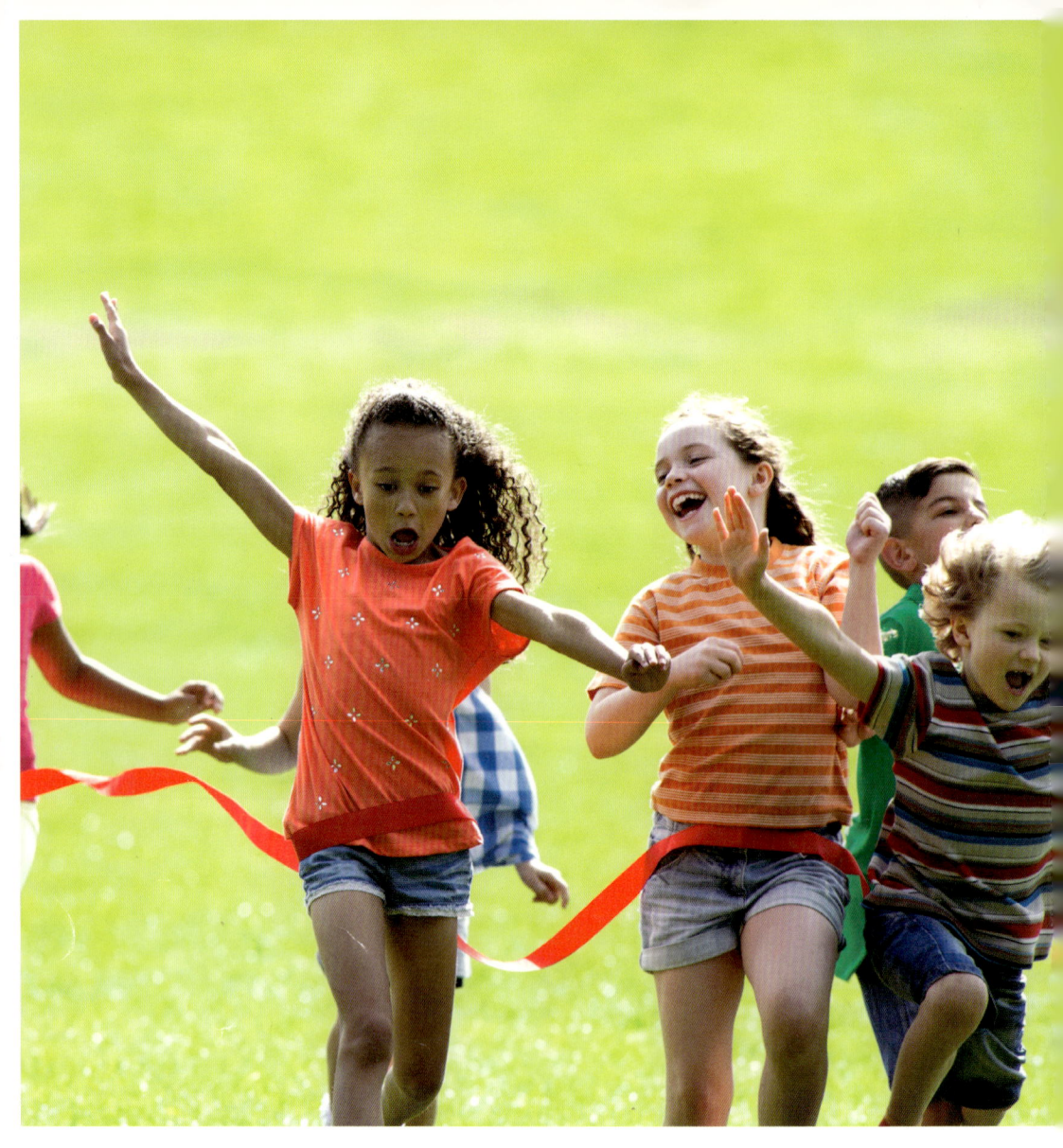

I can run.

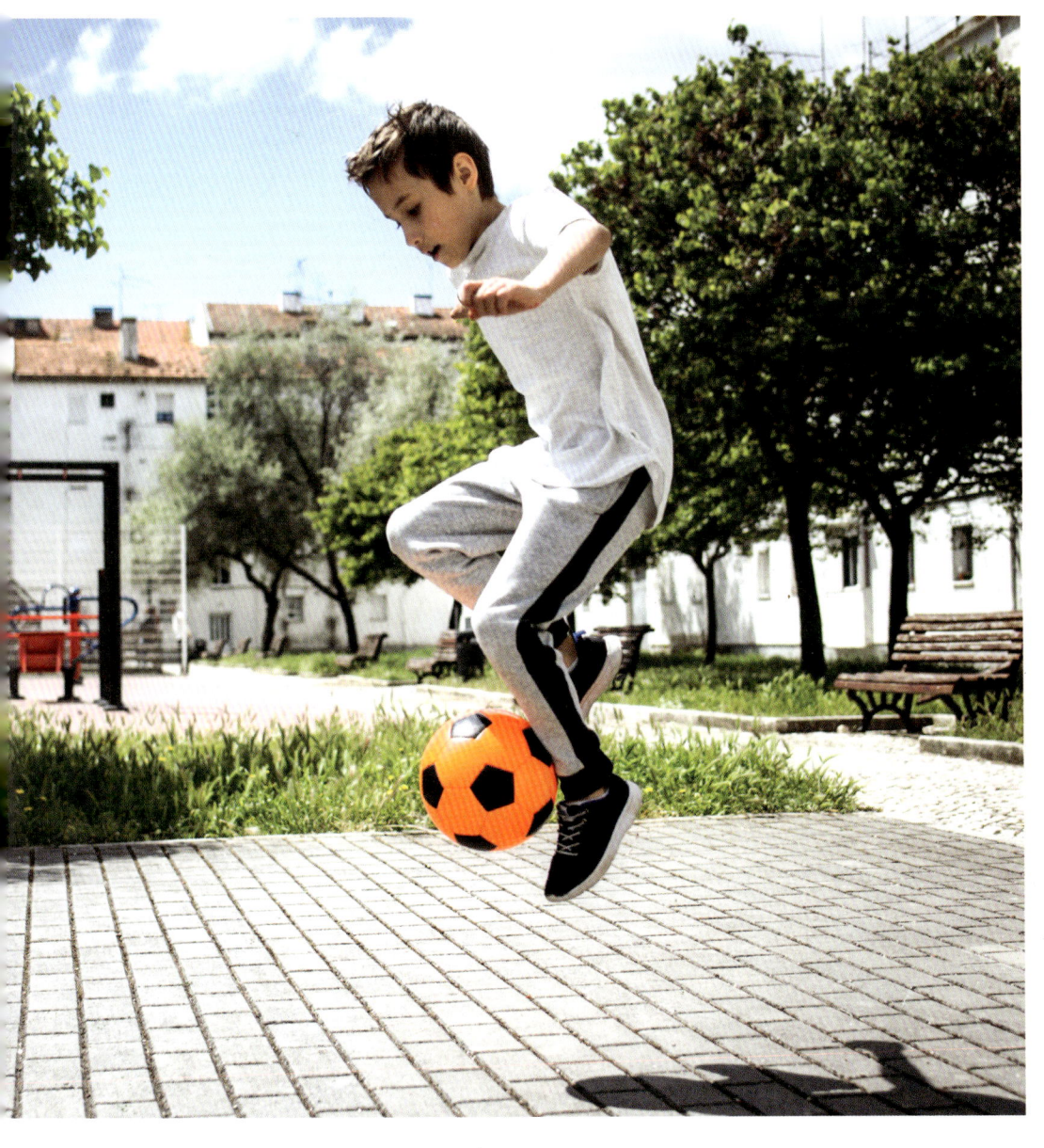

I can run, tug and kick.

I can run

... and tug

... and kick

... in a sack!

I am the tops!

I can get to the top.

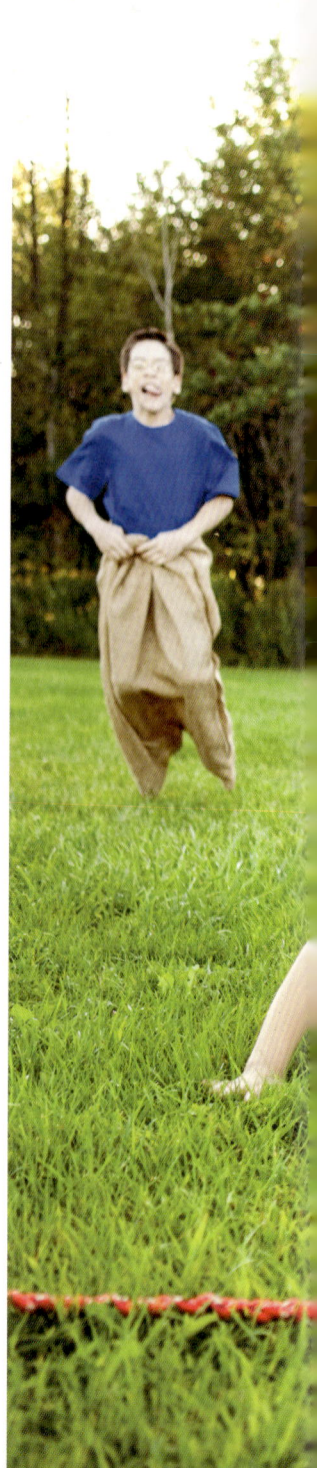

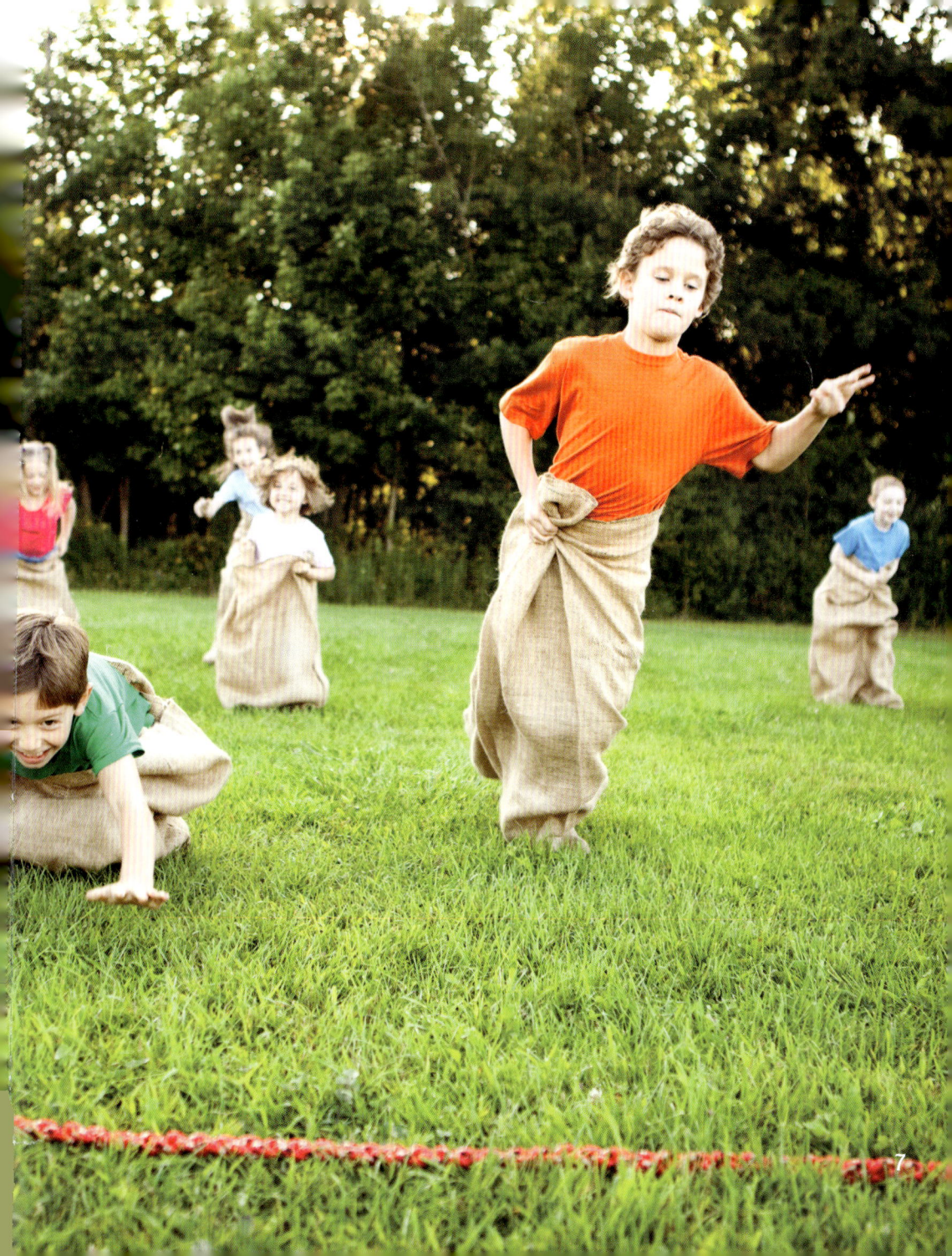

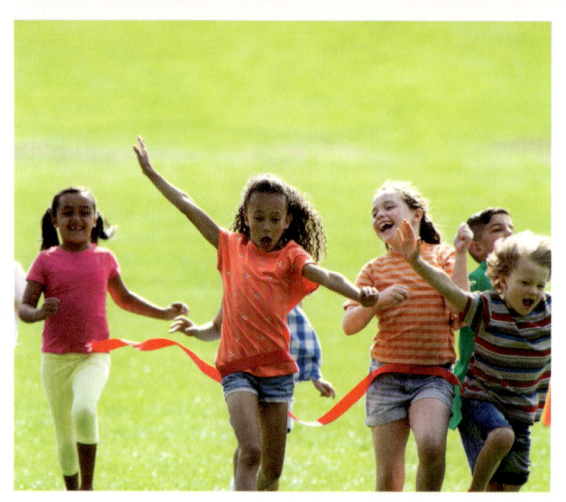
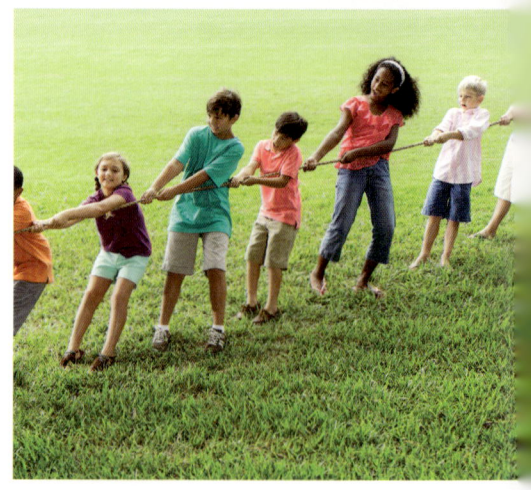
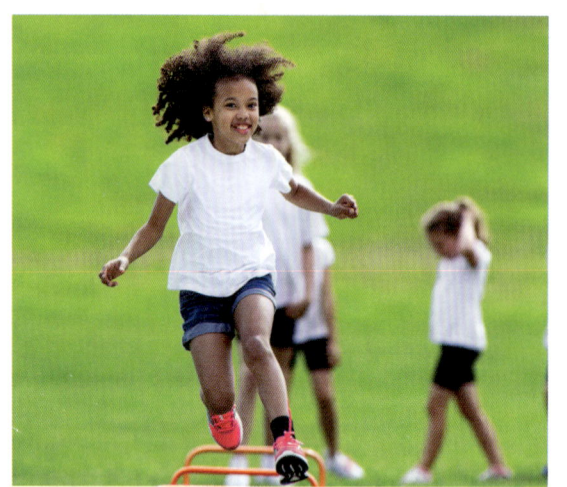
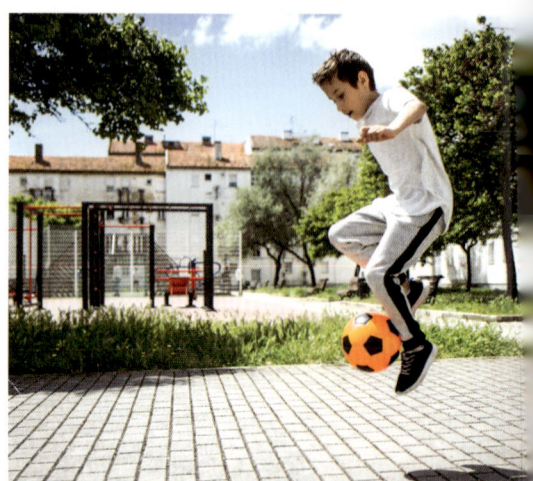

Run, tug.

Run and tug.

Run, tug and kick.